W9-BMN-924

LIGHTNING BOLT BOOKS

# From the Model T to Hybrid Cars

## How Transportation Has Changed

Jennifer Boothroyd

Lerner Publications Company
Minneapolis

For Don—my
favorite travel
companion

Lerner Publications Company
A division of Lerner Publishing Group, Inc.
241 First Avenue North
Minneapolis, MN 55401 U.S.A.

Website address: www.lernerbooks.com


Library of Congress Cataloging-in-Publication Data

Boothroyd, Jennifer, 1972–
     From the Model T to hybrid cars : how transportation has changed / by Jennifer Boothroyd.
     p.    cm. — (Lightning bolt books™—Comparing past and present)
     Includes index.
     ISBN 978-0-7613-6743-7 (lib. bdg. : alk. paper)
     1. Motor vehicles—Juvenile literature. 2. Transportation—Juvenile literature. I. Title.
   TL147.B58  2012
     388—dc22                                                    2011001113

Manufactured in the United States of America
1 — CG — 7/15/11

# Contents

# Transportation

People use transportation to travel from place to place.

Bikes are transportation. Transportation is a tool or method that helps people travel.

Transportation has changed over time.

Bikes used to be bigger and heavier.

# Airplanes

Airplanes fly through the air.

They quickly travel long distances.

In the past, pilots steered airplanes.

These days, pilots often watch over computers that steer airplanes.

# In the past, planes had propellers.

A plane's propellers helped it lift off the ground.

These days, planes are powered by jet engines. They fly much faster.

Jet engines are more powerful than propellers.

In the past, traveling by airplane was very expensive. The planes did not hold many people.

Passengers dressed nicely for a plane trip. They ate fancy meals.

These days, airplane travel is more affordable. More people travel by plane.

Passengers dress more comfortably on airplanes these days.

# Trains

Trains carry people and goods.
Trains run along metal tracks.

In the past, people would eat and sleep on trains. These days, such long train rides are less common.

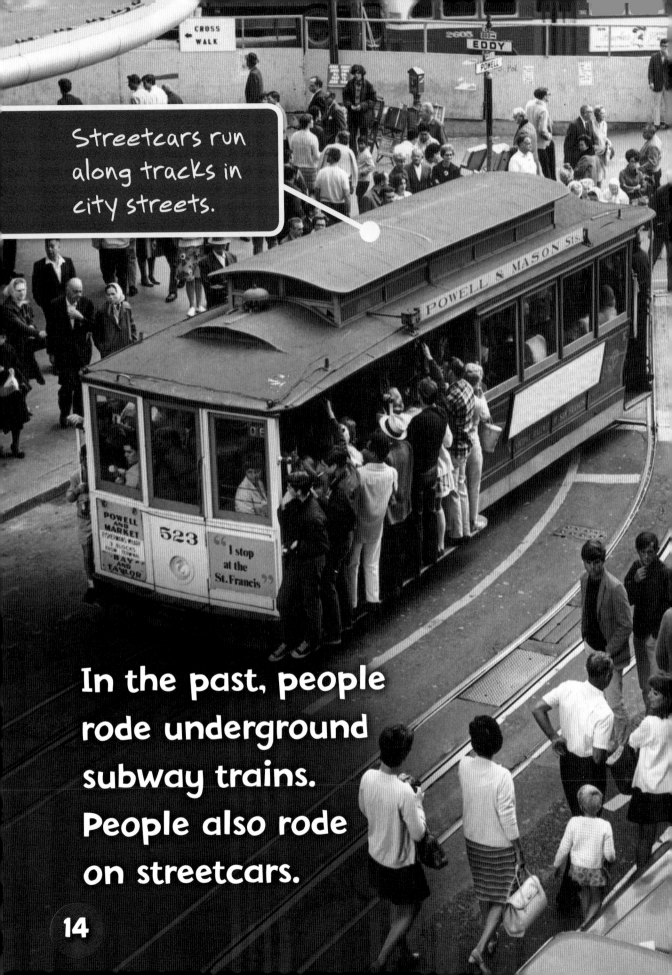

Streetcars run along tracks in city streets.

In the past, people rode underground subway trains. People also rode on streetcars.

These days, people still travel in subway trains. Or they take light-rail trains.

Light-rail trains are faster than streetcars.

People are building faster trains for travel between large cities. Some travelers can ride in high-speed rail trains instead of airplanes.

This high-speed train travels from New York City to Washington, D.C.

# Boats and Ships

People travel across water in boats and ships.

VICTORIA 797

Campion

# In the past, people crossed the ocean in large ships.

Ocean liners were a popular type of passenger ship.

These days, most people choose to fly across the ocean in an airplane. But some people enjoy traveling on cruise ships.

Cruise ships often have restaurants and stores. Some even have ice rinks and movie theaters.

People cross lakes and rivers in canoes and rowboats. These boats have been used in the past and the present.

Early canoes were carved from wood. Modern canoes are made from metal or fiberglass.

# Cars

People travel long and short distances in cars.

In the past, people started cars by turning a crank. Later, people started cars by turning a key.

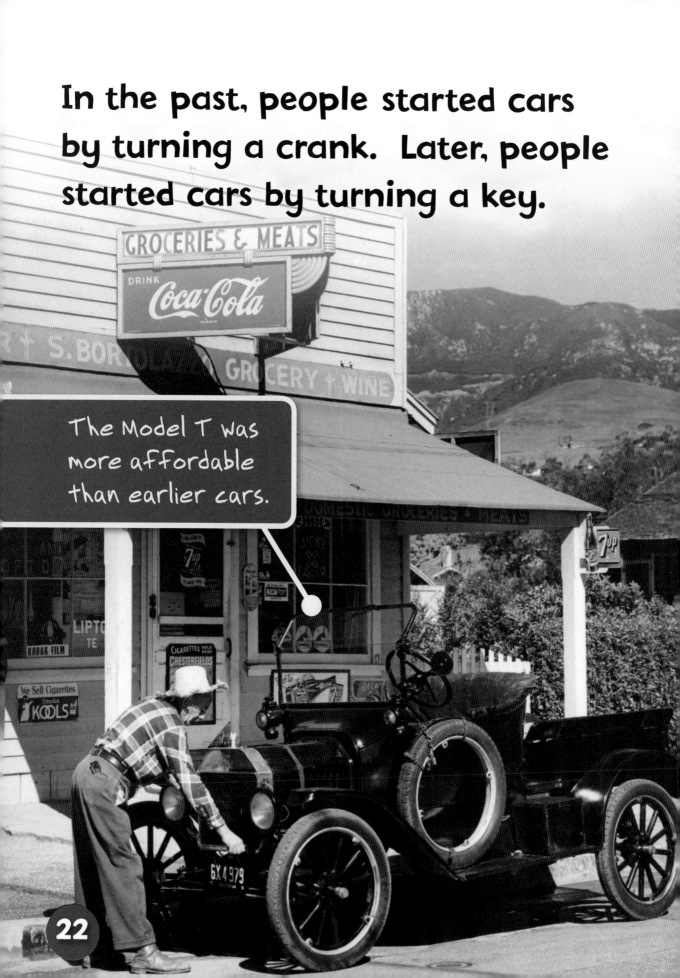

The Model T was more affordable than earlier cars.

# People don't need keys to start some newer cars.

START STOP ENGINE

Pushing a button makes this car start.

In the past, cars did not have seat belts.

# These days, seat belts and car seats keep people safe.

In the past, cars ran on gasoline. Many cars still do. But gasoline engines cause pollution. So people have made hybrid cars that use both gas and electricity.

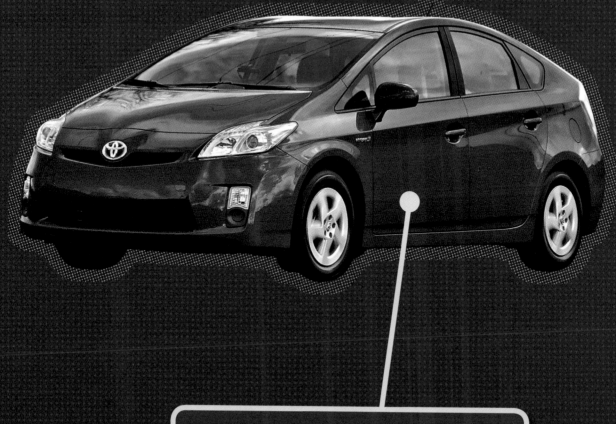

Pollution makes our land, water, or air dirty. Hybrid cars cause less pollution.

The ways people travel have changed with time. But many people still choose to walk when they can. This is the oldest type of transportation.

# Names to Know

These people improved transportation around the world.

**Ole Evinrude:** Ole Evinrude created a popular outboard motor in 1907. Outboard motors hang on the outside of a boat. Ole had worked with gas engines in cars. He thought they could work on boats. He started a company to test and sell motors for water travel.

**Henry Ford:** Henry Ford created the moving assembly line around 1908. Before then, workers put cars together one at a time. With the assembly line, each worker put a separate part on each car that came by. Workers could make cars more quickly than before.

**George Westinghouse:** George Westinghouse invented the air brake for trains in 1869. Before the air brake, stopping a train was tricky. Every train car had a separate brake. With the air brake, people could stop all train cars at once. This made train travel safer.

**The Wright Brothers:** Orville and Wilbur Wright were the first people to fly an aircraft with a motor. Before 1903, no one had built a machine that could fly from off the ground. That year, the brothers flew their motor-powered plane in Kitty Hawk, North Carolina.

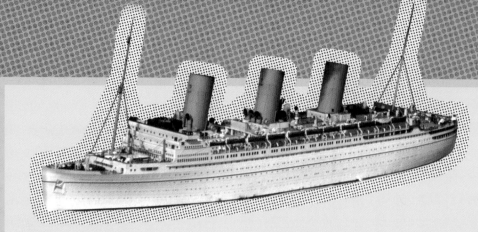

# Glossary

**crank:** a handle that turns in a circle

**distance:** a length of space between two places

**engine:** a machine that turns energy into motion

**gasoline:** a liquid fuel used in some engines

**goods:** things to sell

**hybrid:** a combination of two or more things. Hybrid cars use a combination of gas and electricity.

**light-rail:** a train that moves aboveground across a city

**pollution:** making Earth's land, water, or air dirty

**propeller:** a fan that spins and pushes against water and air

**subway:** a system of trains that travel through tunnels

**transportation:** tools or methods for traveling from place to place

# Further Reading

Heinz, Brian. *Nathan of Yesteryear and Michael of Today.* Minneapolis: Millbrook Press, 2007.

Hill, Lee Sullivan. *Trains on the Move.* Minneapolis: Lerner Publications Company, 2011.

Hodgkins, Fran. *How People Learned to Fly.* New York: HarperCollins, 2007.

National Air and Space Museum: America by Air
http://www.nasm.si.edu/americabyair/flyacross/index.cfm

National Museum of American History: America on the Move
http://americanhistory.si.edu/onthemove/games

# Index

# Photo Acknowledgments

The images in this book are used with the permission of: © Jag_cz/Shutterstock Images, p. 2; © I Love Images/Cultura/Getty Images, p. 4; © Dean Loomis/Time & Life Pictures/Getty Images, p. 5; © Icholakov/Dreamstime.com, p. 6; © Hulton Archive/Getty Images, pp. 7 (top), 29; © Viorel Dudau/Dreamstime.com, p. 7 (bottom); © Superstock/Getty Images, p. 8, 18, 22; © Aleksandar Kolundzija/Vetta/Getty Images, p. 9; © Bettman/CORBIS, p. 10; © ColorBlind Images/Blend Images/Getty Images, p. 11; © Ellen McKnight/Alamy, p. 12; © John Drysdale/Hulton Archive/Getty Images, p. 13; © SuperStock, p. 14; © Jim Parkin/Alamy, p. 15; © Doug Kanter/AFP/Getty Images, p. 16; © maXx images/SuperStock, p. 17; © Buddy Mays/CORBIS, p. 19; © Ariel Skelley/Blend Images/Getty Images, pp. 20, 27; © Elwynn/Dreamstime.com, p. 21; © Image Source/Getty Images, p. 23; © Vintage Images/ReView/Archive Photos/Getty Images, p. 24; © Diane Macdonald/Stockbyte/Getty Images, p. 25; © Bloomberg via Getty Images, p. 26; © Herbert Gehr/Time & Life Pictures/Getty Images, p. 28; © Science and Society/SuperStock, p. 30; © L Barnwell/Shutterstock Images, p. 31.

Front cover: © Michael Shake/Shutterstock Images (hybrid car); © Science and Society/SuperStock (Ford Model T).

Main body text set in Johann Light 30/36.